Quotes...

Ancient Greeks

By
The Secret Libraries

ANCIENT GREEKS QUOTES

"All that is said by any of us can only be imitation and representation."

—Plato

Future ages will wonder at us, as the present age wonders at us now.

—Per...

The Secret Libraries

Published by The Secret Libraries for 2018
www.theSECRETlibraries.com

Contents

This book provides a selected collection of 106 quotes from the works of the greatest ancient Greeks, Find out more about the best philosophers, playwrights, poets, historians, scientists, kings, leaders. Discover more about the thoughts of the following:

Thank you for your purchase!

We spent a long time building this book we hope you enjoy it

"*Do not spoil what you have by desiring what you have not; remember that what you now have was once among the things you only hoped for.*"

— Euripides

"*There is only one good, knowledge, and one evil, ignorance.*"

— Socrates

(Socrates left no writings of his own, the records of his

teachings are from a few ancient authors who referred to him in their own works)

"Men grow tired of sleep, love, singing and dancing sooner than of war"

— Homer

"*For once touched by love, everyone becomes a poet.*"

— Plato

"We ought so to behave to one another as to avoid making enemies of our friends, and at the same time to make friends of our enemies"

— Pythagoras

"For the actuality of thought is *life.*"

— Aristotle

"Thus they let their anger and fury take from them the sense of humanity, and demonstrated that no beast is more savage than man when possessed with power answerable to his rage."

— Plutarch

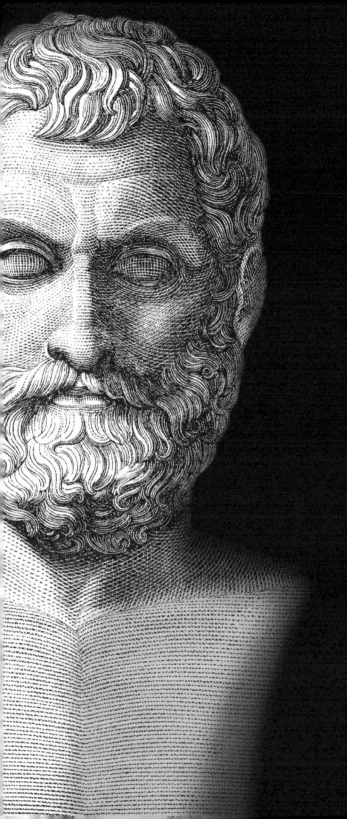

"*Time is the wisest of all things that are; for it brings everything to light*"

— Thales of Miletus

"Are you still to learn that the end and perfection of our victories is to avoid the vices and infirmities of those whom we subdue?"

— Alexander the Great

"He who is not satisfied
with a little,
is satisfied with
nothing"

— Epicurus

"An unlucky rich man is more capable of satisfying his desires and of riding out disaster when it strikes, but a lucky man is better off than him...He is the one who deserves to be described as happy. But until he is dead, you had better refrain from calling him happy, and just call him fortunate"

— Solon

"*It is in the character of very few men to honor without envy a friend who has* **prospered.**"

— Aeschylus

"That the Moon receives its light

from the sun."

— Aristarchus of Samos

" *One word Frees us of all*

the weight and pain of

life: That word is

love"

— Sophocles

"As a matter of self-preservation, a man needs good friends or ardent enemies, for the former instruct him and the latter take him to task."

— Diogenes

"The company of just and righteous men is better than wealth and a rich estate."

— Euripides

"You must learn all things, both the unshaken heart of persuasive truth, and the opinions of mortals in which there is no true warranty."

— Parmenides

"Quickly, bring me a beaker of wine, so that I may wet my mind and say something clever."

— Aristophanes

"It would be better for me... that multitudes of men should disagree with me rather than that I, being one, should be out of harmony with myself."

— Socrates

"*No act of kindness,*

no matter how small,

is ever wasted."

— Aesop

"To a man who has any self-respect, nothing is more dishonourable than to be honoured, not for his own sake, but on account of the reputation of his ancestors."

— Plato

"If you add a little to a little, and then do it again, soon that little shall be much."

— Hesiod

"It is not necessary to ask whether soul and body are one, just as it is not necessary to ask whether the wax and its shape are one, nor generally whether the matter of each thing and that of which it is the matter are one. For even if one and being are spoken of in several ways, what is properly so spoken of is the actuality."

— Aristotle

"The difficulty is not so great
to die for a friend,
as to find a friend worth
dying for."

— Homer

"Good breeding in cattle depends on physical health, but in men on a well-formed character."

— Democritus

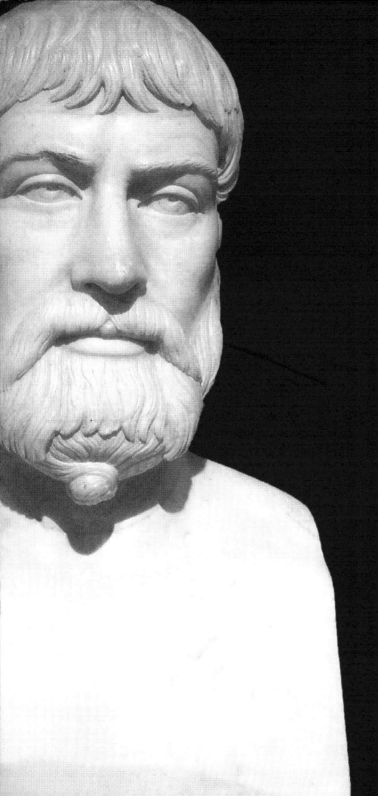

"A graceful and honourable old age is the childhood of immortality."

— Pindar

"*Let no one be slow to seek wisdom when he is young nor weary in the search of it when he has grown old. For no age is too early or too late for the health of the soul.*"

— Epicurus

"*If you are my friend,
stand up before me
and scatter the grace
that's in your eyes.*"

— Sappho of Lesbos

"Wealth I desire to have; but wrongfully to get it, I do not wish. Justice, even if slow, is sure."

— Solon

"*I know that human happiness never remains long in the same place.*"

— Herodotus

"What you leave behind is not what is engraved in stone monuments, but what is woven into the lives of others."

— Pericles

"The secret to happiness is freedom... And the secret to freedom is courage."

— Thucydides

"Our enemies are Medes and Persians, men who for centuries have lived soft and luxurious lives; we of Macedon for generations past have been trained in the hard school of danger and war."

— Alexander the Great

"Give me the place to stand, and I shall move the earth."

— Archimedes

"Cowards do not count in battle; they are there, but not in it."

— Euripides

"*There is no royal road to*

geometry."

— Euclid

"Your lost friends are not dead, but gone before,

advanced a stage or two upon that road which you

must travel in the steps

they trod."

— Aristophanes

"Life is short, and Art long; the crisis fleeting; experience perilous, and decision difficult."

— Hippocrates

"It is indifferent to me where I am to begin, for there shall I return again"

— Parmenides

"Rest satisfied with doing well, and leave others to talk of you as they please."

— Pythagoras

"The first principles of the universe are atoms and empty space; everything else is merely thought to exist."

— Democritus

"There is nothing impossible
to him who will
try."

— Alexander the Great

"Wonder is the feeling of a philosopher, and philosophy begins in wonder."

— Plato

"To advise according to the laws what was best for the people."

— Cleisthenes

"Time is that wherein there is opportunity, and opportunity is that wherein there is no great time."

— Hippocrates

"It is not possible to found a lasting power upon injustice, perjury, and treachery."

— Demosthenes

"Those who claim to discover everything but produce no proofs of the same may be confuted as having actually pretended to discover the impossible."

— Archimedes

"*Future ages will wonder at us, as the present age wonders at us now.*"

— Pericles

"Circumstances rule men; men do not rule circumstances."

— Herodotus

"Marry a good man, and bear good children.."

(In response to his wife's question of what she should do if he died in battle)

— Leonidas I

"Observe due measure, for right timing is in all things the most important factor."

— Hesiod

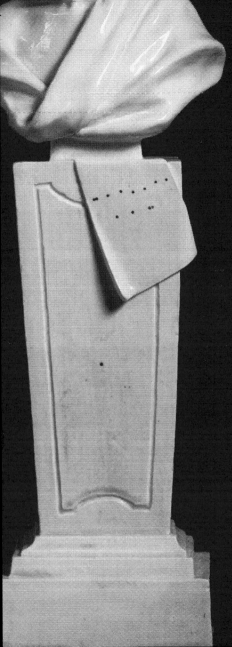

"*No man ever steps in the same river twice, for it's not the same river and he's not the same man.*"

— Heraclitus

"Knowledge of the fact differs from knowledge of the reason for the fact."

— Aristotle

"The mind is not a vessel to be filled but a fire to be kindled."

— Plutarch

"As to diseases, make a habit of two things — to help, or at least, to do no harm."

— Hippocrates

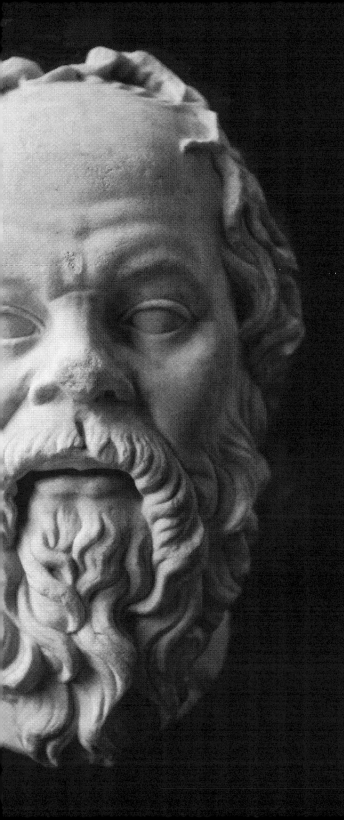

"The unexamining life is not worth living for a human being."

— Socrates

"The easiest thing in the world is self-deceit; for every man believes what he wishes, though the reality is often different."

— Demosthenes

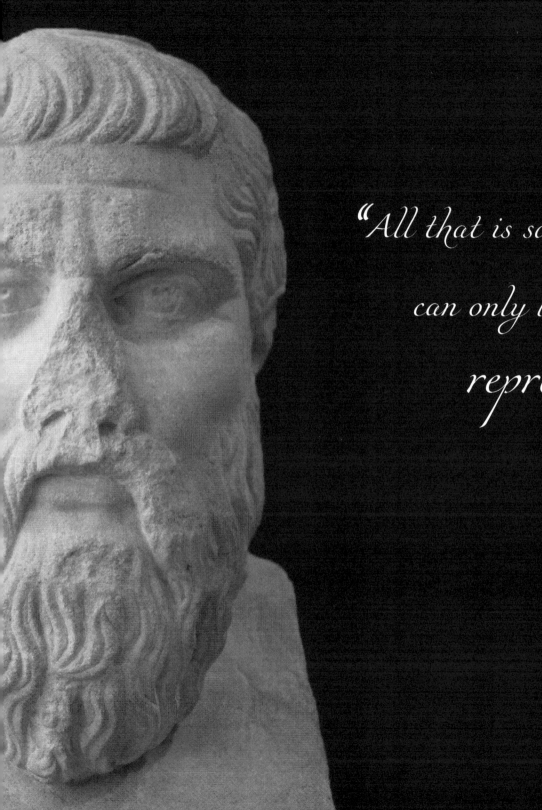

"*All that is said by any of us
can only be imitation and
representation.*"

— Plato

"Rule, after you have first learned to

submit to rule."

— Solon

"Knowledge of the fact differs from knowledge of the reason for the fact."

— Aristotle

"We hang the petty thieves and appoint the great ones to public office."

— Aesop

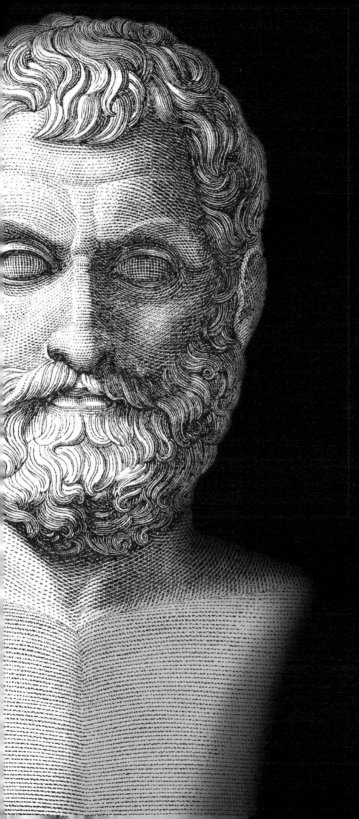

"Water is the first principle

of everything"

— Thales of Miletus

"So little pains do the vulgar take in the investigation of truth, accepting readily the first story that comes to hand."

— Thucydides

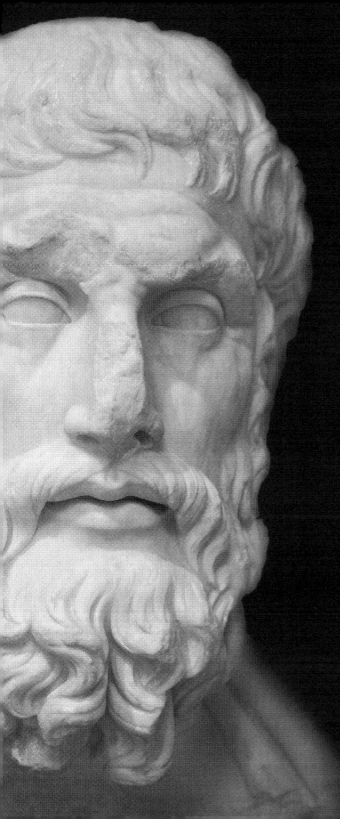

"Self-sufficiency is the greatest of all wealth."

— Epicurus

"The unexamining life is not worth living for a human being."

— Socrates

"A prosperous fool is a grievous burden."

— Aeschylus

"Virginity, virginity, when you leave me, where do you go?

I am gone and never come back to you.

I never return."

— Sappho of Lesbos

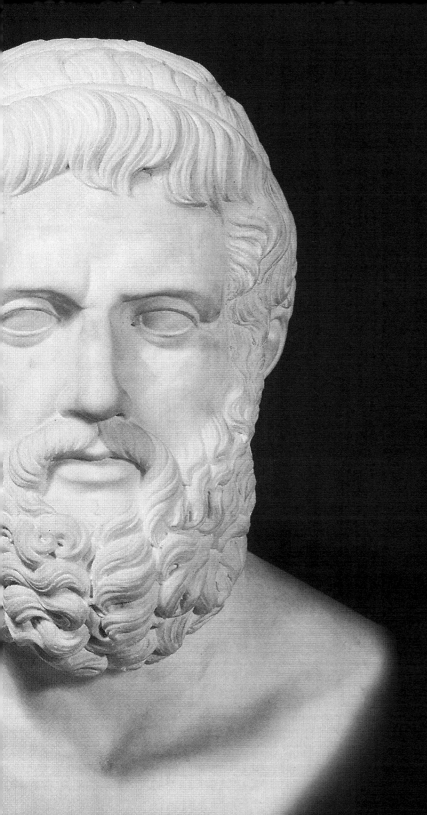

"*Always desire to learn something useful.*"

— Sophocles

"The animal needing something knows how much it needs, the man does not."

— Democritus

"Hope is the only good that is common to all men; those who have nothing else possess hope still"

— Thales of Miletus

"*A man may learn wisdom even from a foe.*"

— Aristophanes

"Freedom is the sure possession of those alone who have the courage to defend it."

— Pericles

"*Gratitude is the sign of noble souls.*"

— Aesop

"That city in which those who are not wronged, no less than those who are wronged, exert themselves to punish the wrongdoers."

— Solon

one is a great blessing."

— Hesiod

"No man can tell what the future may bring forth, and small opportunities are often the beginning of great enterprises."

— Demosthenes

"A guest never forgets the host who has treated him kindly."

— Homer

"Holy shadows of the dead, I'm not to blame for your cruel and bitter fate, but the accursed rivalry which brought sister nations and brother people, to fight one another. I do not feel happy for this victory of mine. On the contrary, I would be glad, brothers, if I had all of you standing here next to me, since we are united by the same language, the same blood and the same visions."

— Alexander the Great

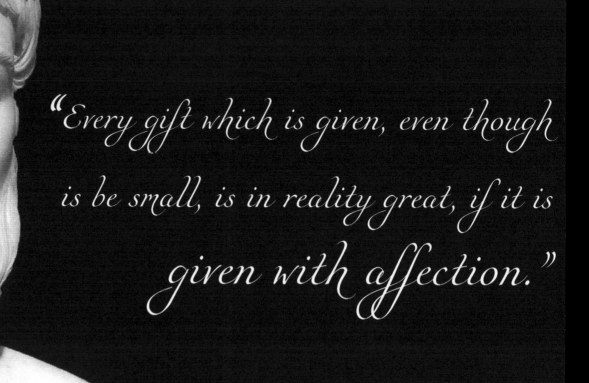

"Every gift which is given, even though is be small, is in reality great, if it is given with affection."

— Pindar

"Conclusions which are merely verbal cannot bear fruit, only those do which are based on demonstrated fact."

— Hippocrates

"A handsome man guards his Image a while; a good man will one day take on beauty."

— Sappho of Lesbos

"The foundation of every state is the education of its youth."

— Diogenes

"Men trust their ears less than their eyes."

— Herodotus

"*In every tyrant's heart there springs in the end.*

This poison, that he cannot

trust a friend."

— Aeschylus

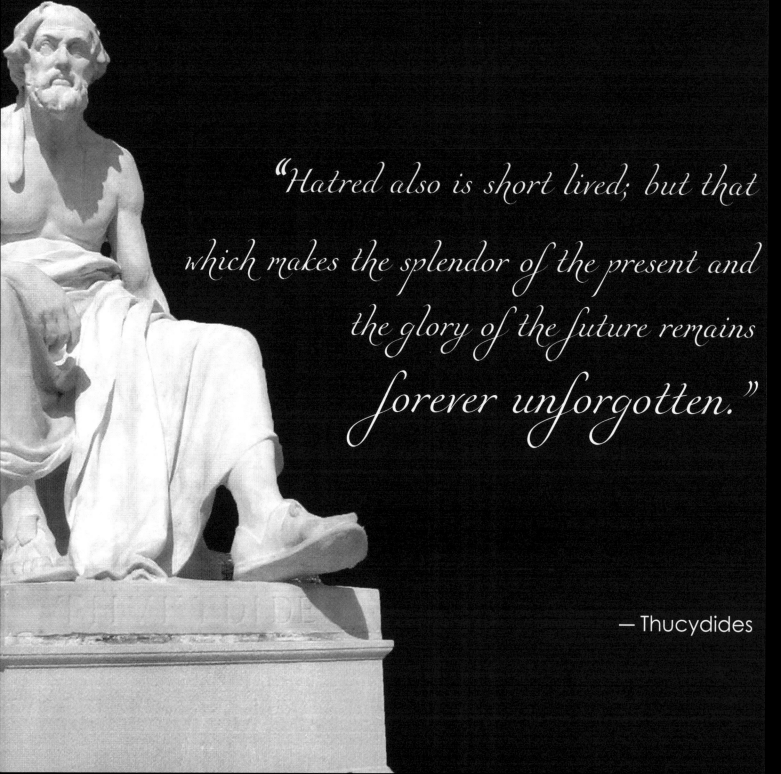

"Hatred also is short lived; but that which makes the splendor of the present and the glory of the future remains forever unforgotten."

— Thucydides

"Universal is known according to reason, but that which is particular, according to sense...."

— Aristotle

"*(I have found it!)*

Eureka!."

— Archimedes

"All that is said by any of us can only be imitation and representation."

— Plato

"Give him threepence, since he must make gain out of what he learns."

— Euclid

"I only wish that wisdom were the kind of thing that flowed ... from the ressel that was full to the one that was empty."

— Socrates

"*Everything in excess is opposed to nature.*"

— Hippocrates

"The brave man is not only he who overcomes the enemy, but he who is stronger than pleasures. Some men are masters of cities, but are enslaved to women."

— Democritus

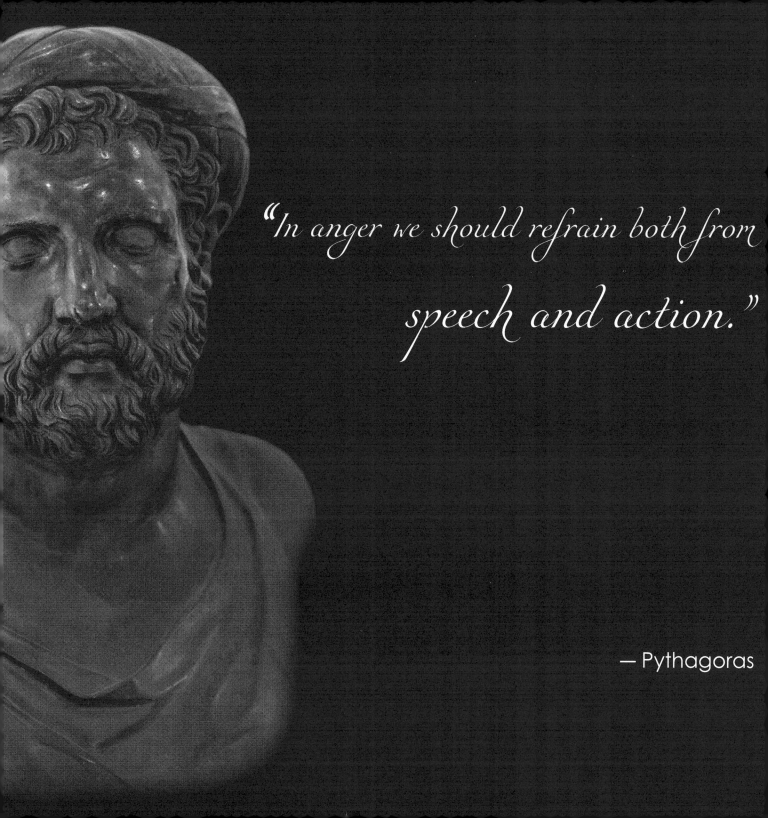

"In anger we should refrain both from speech and action."

— Pythagoras

"Avoid doing what you would blame others for doing."

— Thales of Miletus

"*I do not steal*

victory."

— Alexander the Great

"*No man is hurt but by himself.*"

— Diogenes

"*Every advantage in the past is judged in the light of the final issue.*"

— Demosthenes

"Arrogance in full bloom bears a crop of ruinous folly from which it reaps a harvest all of tears."

— Aeschylus

"*Although only a few may originate a policy, we are all able to judge it.*"

— Pericles

"Success is dependent on effort."

— Sophocles

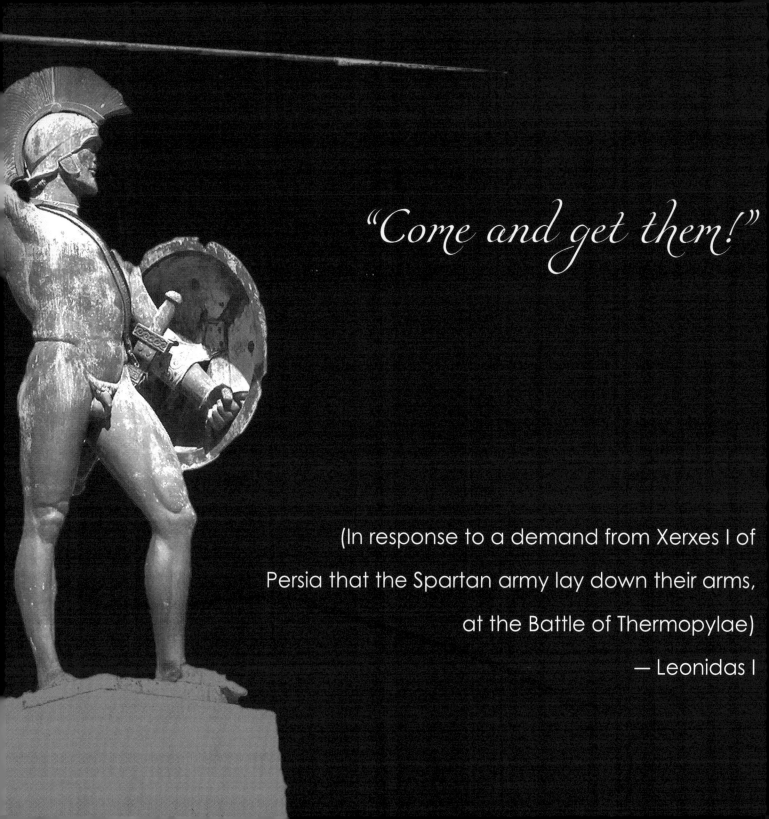

"Come and get them!"

(In response to a demand from Xerxes I of Persia that the Spartan army lay down their arms, at the Battle of Thermopylae)

— Leonidas I

"Men of sense often learn from their enemies. It is from their foes, not their friends, that cities learn the lesson of building high walls and ships of war."

— Aristophanes

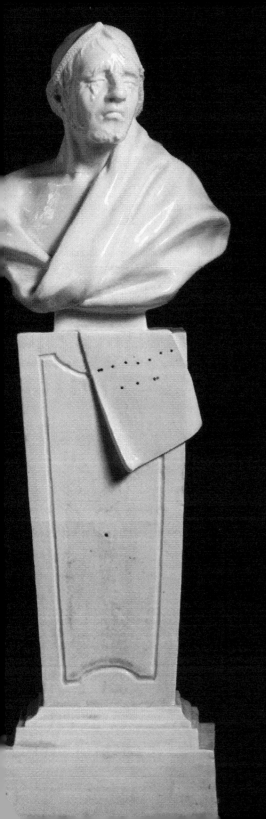

"*There is nothing permanent*

Except change."

— Heraclitus

"Hateful to me as the gates of Hades is that man who hides one thing in his heart and speaks another."

— Homer

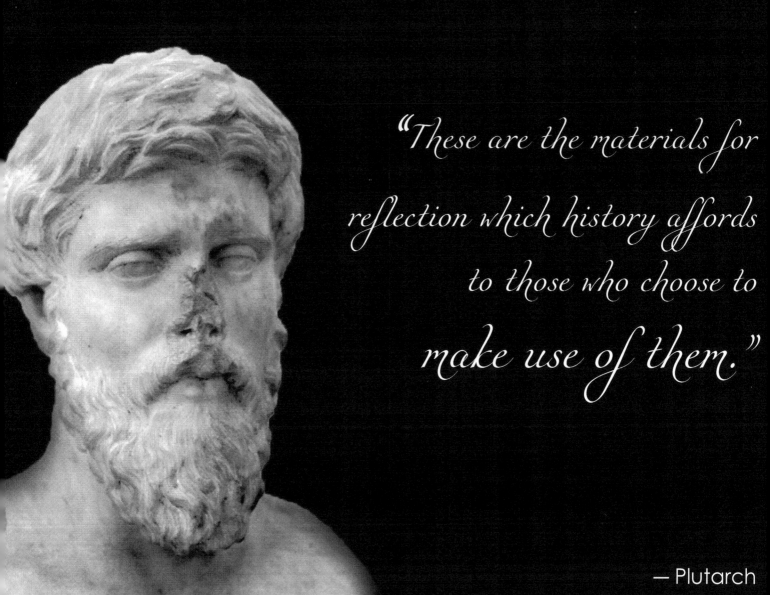

"These are the materials for reflection which history affords to those who choose to make use of them."

— Plutarch

Thank you for your purchase!

We spent a long time building this book.

We hope you enjoyed it :)

If you did please help us by leaving a review...

PS. Join our team to receive some Kindle edition books free and before anyone else...

Find out more on our website here:

www.thesecretlibraries.com

The Secret Libraries

Published by The Secret Libraries for 2017
www.theSECRETlibraries.com

Manufactured by Amazon.ca
Bolton, ON